I0150700

ONE HOUSE LEFT STANDING:
A Book of Poetry

By

Ryan Fredric Steinbeck

© 2009 by Ryan Fredric Steinbeck.
All rights reserved. No part of this book may be reproduced, stored in a retrieval system, or transmitted in any form by any means without prior written permission of the publisher, except by a reviewer who may quote brief passages in a review to be printed in a newspaper, magazine or journal.

First Printing.

ISBN: 978-0-578-00494-5

Thank You:

Thank you to my family, relatives, extended family. You all know who you are. Thanks to Mike Steinbeck for another great cover. Thank you to Heather and Adam Gemmer for the back cover photo.

ACKNOWLEDGEMENTS

I assume acknowledgements are a thank you to those who have inspired me. My wife, my family, my friends and all of their situations are part of this book. My poems develop out of your good, and yes, your bad times. Success, failure, loss, and new life are all inspirations for me. So, I guess what I'm trying to say is, thank you for living your life.

Politics, the state of the planet and environment, good and evil and all things in between are also part of this book.

Also thanks to the poets, musical artists, and writers out there. A great movie, song, poem, or story in general can inspire me, and has done so more times than I can count. Without these artists, I would have never believed I could be one myself, and more importantly, I never would have tried.

TABLE OF CONTENTS:

The following poems have been written over a very complex few years. I was picked up by someone who forced me to know my true self and who allowed me to exorcise my demons. She sacrificed a lot in this process. Eventually I realized she was the only one brave enough to tell me the truth. She is the most important part of my life, keeping me grounded and honest. Through her, I learned the meaning of unconditional love. She taught me life is about ending my fear and facing another person who demands something more of you than you could ever demand of yourself. This book is for my wife, Cindy.

TO THE READER:

First of all, thank you for showing enough interest to have opened this book. I just wanted to advise you that I have divided this book into two sections. The first, called the *Living Room*, is mostly about love. The second, called the *Meditation Room*, is about all other subjects. This was an inspiration loosely derived from my grandfather-in-law, who wondered where the happy poems about his granddaughter were. He has been waiting for a little more uplifting book. I wanted to make them easily accessible to him, and anyone else who didn't always want to try and decipher the topics of these poems. I attempted to make this book a little more reader friendly. I'm always open to these suggestions.

Thank you,

Ryan

LIVING ROOM

ONE HOUSE LEFT STANDING SECTION I

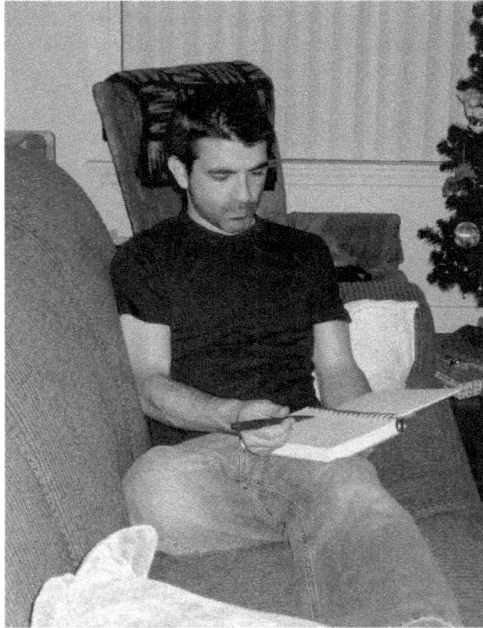

35

Time is an odd thing
Gradually adding trepidation
Complicating more than conveying
Speaking more than listening
Confusing instead of enlightening
Demanding a mark instead of allowing mistakes
Urging success and threatening failure
Bringing on retrospect
Hallucination of reminisce
Petitioning survival
I was so many things at one time
That was so many years ago
I can't remember what I tried to be
Or what I was so disappointed for
When that world closed on me

An hourglass
With less sand on top than on bottom
Little in the way of sympathy
From anyone with any more
I'm not running on empty
I haven't been regret
I don't need consideration
I don't want to forget
I don't want to make excuses
I'm not guided by fear
I'm not ready to lie down and die
It's just another year

ONE HOUSE LEFT STANDING

A gentle breeze and consequent rain
The howl now a whisper
Everything turns to calm
Welcome to the aftermath

The largest natural disaster
Complete annihilation
I shuffle through the ruins
Looking for some hope

Under the overpass
Over the feelings
Once upon a time
In a fairy tale

It feels like a different life
Like ancestors looking at history books
Not desensitized but through the renovation
Surprised by how different the same thing appears

She just happened across my mind
On a day when I was going to decide
She failed to bring up anything she put down
The person she knew is no longer around

Southward through path of the storm
My relentlessness evident on every turn
I became tired of starting again
Much too long ago

I'm outside of the sorrow
I make a path through the demolition
Knowing it is better
On the other side

A voice inside my head
Listened to a possibility
Creating a ray of hope
Shining through the darkness

Continuing on my way
Watching the world recreate
Picking up the pieces
Looking for a sign of life

Approaching from the west
Eventually my sight is challenged
I reach the point of landfall
The stories were true

Beyond the devastation
On the distant shoreline
One structure still stands in view
From here it appears like new

Signs of exterior damage
But the pillars and foundation appear strong
In need of some restoration
It shouldn't be too long

Time to end an era
To release the burden carried
To forgive all failures and mistakes
To find a ray of the sun

A vision out of focus
Has now come into view
I found one house left standing
Inside I found you

RECONSTRUCTION: (One House Left Standing part II)

It began today
Just as the eastern sky caught fire
Neighbors once strangers
Working as one
Filling the spaces
Changing the world
Keeping track of honor
Deeds without recognition
Tasks without request
A bond unspoken
They've all been through this before
They believe in karma
They've been in need
Now it's time for them
As someday it will be for me
It may take years before it's over
But the reconstruction begins today

FROM THE GROUND UP (One House Left Standing part III)

Heart and mind reassembled
Feet back on the ground
Legs put together in place
Scaffolding used for limbs
The head returns from the clouds
After the retreat
A new mind of thinking installed
Heart beats at a different rhythm
Soul installed to seek solace
I'm rebuilt from the ground up

WINTER

Empty house shares my echo
Time brings one last emotion before sleep
All day I need more than I should need
In the heart of winter there are no more leaves

Another road paves over everything
It's not by chance you and I are here
I was willing to transcend time
I feel winter in your heart and stare

Your voice echoes in fragments
The coldest days remain
The night whispers memories
Reminding me when winter set you free

OUR SPRING

I feel the warm sun on my face
I hear the drips of melting snow
On this roof top I see forever
A semblance of peace within the world

Warmest day of the season
Internalized as I lie here
Silence fills the calm around me
I'm close to understanding

Out of society's view
Though much development is before me
I'd like to slow down and appreciate
Before my time is through

I feel the sunny days inside you
Even though I tried to crush the joy it brings
If summer is our perfect happiness
I think we've finally reached our spring

SUMMER DAY

Senses enhanced
With fear on my side
It was rising from me
Like fog in a morning swamp

Along the tragic haughtiness
That marks the road I drive
I fumble through the thoughts in my head
At least I know I'm alive

The majestic sorrow wins awards
The patron forgets what he is fighting for
In the end it's just one of those days
Those days just don't happen anymore

Now I'm left to tell the ending
Of a story I never read
The soul survivor of pretending
All of the other has-been's are dead

A paraphrase of my history
As my mind trails away
Entering selective memory
A rebuttal of myopia on display

Today I feel the warmth
Something resembling a stranger
In its arms it holds me
Protecting me from danger

The shuffling of feet
Cannot deny this new dawn
Those who denied this peace
Have now come and gone

Once a clouding of my eyes
The steam begins to rise
As winter and spring pass through
I just want to spend a summer day with you

A SECRET I NEED TO TELL

I have a secret I need to tell
Why do I want to keep it?
You shouldn't need to wonder
Or brace for intensification

Trouble facing the facts
Before there was nothing
Push the envelope
And it becomes something

It's a matter of taking it for granted
The mind requests a challenge
It's a test I can't win
Not this time

I have a secret I want to tell
I know you know I'll tell you
I just always want your suspense before
And your surprise after

HARVEST OF DREAMS

One particular thing
That happened to you and me
Was in the harvest of my dreams

Mettle as we will
In the ways of supposed to be
In the harvest of my dreams

I was someone's pain
I was fooled and taken in
I will return the next year
When the harvest comes again

Settle into belief
Don't believe all that you see
In the harvest of your dreams

Capture your greatest joys and fears
You are as content as you will ever be
In the harvest of your sweet dreams

OH MY, WHAT A WONDERFUL DAY!

Oh my, what a wonderful day this is!
The circus clowns come up to bat
I've let the yellow customs past
In a sudden shifting from right to left

Like an octopus I have eight arms of love
I've found the alien in disguise
Like a cat he leaps out of his skin
Oh my, what a wonderful day this is!

The family of walls keeps me in my place
Her mind attacks me and then bounces away
It's louder than anything she could say
I've eluded the spectators for today

Monsters hide in the shadows
One glimpse and it would be lethal
This time I was able to get away
Oh my, what a wonderful day!

Shots fired and one round left
Closer to my derivation than I've ever been
Just a word from you and I apprehend
Oh my, what a wonderful day this is!

THE DISTANCE BETWEEN US

Time and distance to you
The unrelenting minutes
Once made contemptuous by the egocentric world
Welcome my imminent ardor

The scars of my endurance
Have been covered with new certainty
The earth is no longer empty
As it embraces the warmth of the sun

Once upon a time
Not so long ago
I thought the flowers would never bloom again
Today I lie in a field of roses

Lost in smokescreens and facades
When the genuine article slipped in the back door
Jump-starting my circulation
When I thought I was dying of starvation

A universal alleviation
For whatever is ailing
A disguise unmasked
With a final revealing

All that was missing
Safe in one location
Unlike anything I've ever been told
The distance between us is just road

A vendetta no longer pursued
A sea that cannot be emptied
A sad narrative no longer told
This time the only distance between us is road

I HAVE ALWAYS KNOWN

In this wayfarers imprisonment
Should chance cause my decent
The only thing that has been meant
I have always known

In the quandaries that have gone
In the shackles where I belong
There is only one true song
I have always known

Time is shortening
All uncertainty vanishing
Soon the world will hear me sing
I have always known

Before the fire light stories come true
Many battles I've been through
All evidence points to you
I have always known

Ever fades the ancient curse
Not drowning but still immersed
There were others but you are first
I have always known

NEW DIRECTION

Sleeping with all I take for granted
I attempt to open my eyes
It used to be a challenge
You can have the last laugh this time

I used to expect the unexpected
Until I expected something more
I knew there would never be another way
A truth I chose to ignore

I winterized my heart for a long time
I knew I couldn't escape the snow
I was forsaken after your blizzard
Until I found a lantern's warm glow

Through the liturgy that was once you and I
I relinquish my mind's protection
I clear the exit for the last time
With my heart pointed in a new direction

THROUGH HEAD AND HEART

There are always two routes
One through my head
The other through my heart
Neither passage is unexploited
Both have seen better days
Both have been in decline

Please watch for the road signs
There are caveats all the way
Many closed exits
Countless construction lanes
You should know which way to turn
From accidents caused by those gone astray
With wreckage and decay

All of the greatest sufferers
Analogous complaints
My heart believes in something
While my head does the conflicting
There's a battle of the obdurate
Envious of sabotage

My head usually fights to the end
On what my heart decides
History has trouble accepting
That anything could go right
Patience could lead to revelations
You could be a revelation

Within my heart's sincerity
Battles endure into night
Falling asleep before its time
I miss the final confrontation
Optimistic for the outcome
Tomorrow is a new day

My heart knows what it knows
It knows what is true
After hours of negotiations
Battles I win and lose
In the end my heart won over
The final transcriptions are on record
For the first time in history
There is an avenue to pursue
My heart and head have agreed on something
That something is you

ONWARD

I know which way the wind blows
Where the dust has settled
As I float comfortably
In my sea of change

I'm taking these steps
I'm the ringleader behind this movement
This is my protestation
There is no more fabrication

I find you empyreal
As everything falls into place
Almost too decidedly precise
A reality abiding

Beyond the illusion
That you pull the strings
That somehow I would listen
To anything other than my heart

Your eyes are palliative
Your soul the link to mine
There is nothing left to contemplate
As we take the next step onward

MY ELEMENT

Wide-open road
60 miles to go
Although my feet must wander
My heart is finally at rest

This fire burns
Throughout my institution
The monsters and demons have died
Only you on the inside

The rudiments of shadows cast
From disaster there's recovery
From storms I need shelter
I know where to go now

Fields of wire and metal
Streams of iron and soot
Sky of acid and smoke
You are my element

SHE LIVES IN MY HEAD

Content in this moment
Expansion eternal
Exalted gloriole is my life
Disparage the non-believer I used to be

Escaped from it before
Then trapped in disbelief
I know more than I think
Imputed by lack of grief

I opened the door
She walked right through
My inamorato
She lives in my head

I visit the other limbs
I've gone great distances
I create a supplemental life
She lives in my head

The plague to end all plagues
In need of corruption
The great testament of our time
Headed in my direction

We are a destined journey
No secrets left unsaid
This is the final vowing
She lives in my head

PEOPLE ARE DIFFERENT

The space between us
I stare at your back from the other side of the bed
Feeling like a nightmare
Swimming against the tide

People are different when there's challenge
They turn into what they were before
Even if they escaped it long ago
The paths cross again

I gage your reaction
How I should respond?
I'm a trespasser
On sacred ground

So close but so far
Burned by distant fire
Aware of your weapons and defenses
Hoping someday they will tire

I missed the boat of knowledge
I may never be what you need
I can't compete with your memory
Or how you want things to be

So the nighttime turns up again
If this distance should return
I might never find myself
In time to save us both

It would be an eerie deliverance
Of new befalling old
The old being too familiar
Seemingly eternal

Yet people are different
When I think she has defected
There's an optimism that awaits her tomorrow
It's always better than expected

CYNTHIANA

Cynthiana is beautiful at night
All the stars reflect on her streets
The lights show off like Christmas
As my heart skips a beat

I was out in the depths of space
I turned around and made it home
The only city visible from that distance
All along I should have known

A warmth constantly embracing
A smile on every face
A good deed for the world
A feeling I can't replace

Never to leave the love I found
There isn't anywhere else
Cynthiana found the beauty in me
When I couldn't find it in myself

NOVEMBER

Look on the horizon
There is always something to use
Take a step backward
Or continue to refuse

Manipulation of what can be altered
Or acceptance of truth
Walk forward when they call your name
This time the world is for you

I've been here a long time
Standing without a clue
Waking up one morning
To find the world is new
A break in the clouds
With the sky a deepened blue
A day like no other
Distance in full view

November reveals its secrets
With certain attitude
Aspects of contravention
Precognitive queues

Standing at a confession
With confusion in recluse
The insolubility and uncertainty
All but defused

From November to November
Fiction became truth
Every November
A celebration of this proof

LOVE OF MY LIFE

Time heals all wounds
Never the lesser with misfortune
My waiting for the perfect attempt
Ended when the message began

Now it's an establishment
Building towards a revolution
Here you are and just like a phenomenon
Truth is still a nuisance

Scattered pieces on the pavement
Resembles a life once much different
A new regime in control
After a successful transition

The hindsight begins
Trying to confine
Emotional survival of the fittest
The voids have destabilized

On a tarnished background where the colors have run
Lies a picture that was once just one
You have returned the contrast
Changing dimensions and eradicating the past
Here we stand in a frame together
Captured in this instant
Soon to perpetuate itself
As previous pictures fade

Incarcerate this instant
Like your favorite portrait
Live in the frame evermore
Solidify the borders
Leave the world outside
Our expressions speak volumes
Never to leave our threshold of souls
Just when I thought there was nothing left
A promise until my very last breath
Love of my life
I'll love you until death

ESCAPE

What is this dawning of the new day?
What is this feeling?
The world turns before my eyes
My tide of solace rises

It becomes a stream
Leading to my ocean
I walk on water
As I embrace this belief

Nothing is impossible
With the sun visible at this angle
My breath is the edge of my enlightenment
Slowly inching towards it

Time is a figment of imagination
Time is all we have
Escaping from fear and shame
Is the dawning of my new day

BEAUTIFUL

When my heart was held for ransom
You were the negotiator
In exile I crept from the shadows
You showed me mercy in tragedy

I don't mean to be unwonted
I couldn't help watching you sleep
Every part beautiful
Inside and out

I cherish every instant
In a time when you are peaceful
Every toss and turn
Life is perfect in moments

I cannot be close enough
I cannot know too much
This is where nothing is better
I hope I never forget

In a time of such innocence
I want to protect you from the world
Every part hopeful
Every day surreal

In a footrace to the finish
I take a step backwards
I find no sense in the rush
With you right here

I don't mean to be cliché
I don't mean to not know what to say
Every aspect given
Every aspect received

To aid my grievances
Dispersed throughout my mired past
The undulation of trust
Has washed it all away

Now I see certainty
Ignited by the fire of belief
The coals have been ever so still
Never have they gone cold

I have seen magnificence
I warren in this feeling
I want to be here in between breaths
As time slips through fingers

FILLING THE GAPS

Something outlandish about the north wind
Sending my mind south
A deliberate fascination
Causal celebration
Your true colors show
And they match mine

Fancying a dance with premeditation
Eventual desolation
Sands of time challenge me
To make a decision

There's a message here, somewhere
I read face value's distraction
The pages inside are a homing device
Leading me to your secret side

What can I take away?
What can I give?
What's done is done
Truth escaped everyone
Except the moon and sun
We are the moon and the sun

I see a dream of a reality
I still see your face as you're standing there
As I'm walking towards the door
I know things will never be the same

Time exits the equation
Innocence loses the scuffle
I made friendship with indecision
I've never been more certain

My daydreams stop me in my tracks
I cannot help but to smile
You're the mile markers on my mind's open road
Urging me to pull over for a while

Thank you for changing the wind's direction
For setting me free from myself
You fill the gaps in my thinking
It couldn't have been anyone else

BLINDING LIGHT

Constitution shifting
In this time of giving
Now we all gather
In a different way
A feeling of the feelings
Stillness and calm
Peace in the air
While war continues on
For one day things settle
The mind can travel elsewhere
Other feelings attended to
As we gain strength from one another

You are beautiful inside
You are beautiful out
Others have been myopic
Not to ever see it
You live with the disappointment
You live with the doubt
You live with the fear
That should have been theirs
You are the stronger one
To play the martyr like you do
To pick up the difference
As they try and take advantage of you

No more will this persist
The truth has always been there
You've constantly been my vision
You begin to understand the potentiality
Fear and doubt come together
Creating a force in you
Like a part of your inherited make up
Lying dormant for years

Now you will rise
Above what they can handle
It's your turn to be a blinding light
Instead of just a candle

CONNECTED

A cataclysmic event
Astronomic proportions
I didn't feel myself slipping
As the sound gets louder
The intensity crucifies me
Behind is fallow and unaffected
Because of you
I stand perfected

A prescribed dosage
Distilled
Too potent
Addict and pusher
Diplomat and dignitary
The colors are the same
Reflecting in the sun
You are the strength that fortifies
Heaven cried before
The tears have since dried
Two souls intertwined
Now nothing takes your place

I hear the night talking
About the days slipping away
We no longer listen

You are innate
You are reaction
You are the first nerve that I feel
You are the moral of every story
The center of every thought
Waking hours spent thankful
I stand before you grateful

I have all but slipped under
The question of you
In the name of intensity
I relinquish control

You found me broken
You found me misused
Now I am connected
It's all because of you

STRONGER TOMORROW

Over the last ridge of the last hill
A fire burns the remaining walls down
The misty rain brings no assistance

Still cold in my surroundings
Enclosed in a comfort of ends and beginnings
I want to put my life here

For the end of the year and the end of the world
Time is never forgiving
The misty rain forms your shape

Time documented by the lines on my face
The truths will discover me eventually
I will keep moving

The fire may still burn, but the flood is no longer
My home is here with you today
Tomorrow it will be stronger

VERGE

Spending, rolling, unfolding
The ground spreads out underfoot
Laying claim to the new day
As the arc of light is gracious
You are around tonight
Like the first vision into perception
The light is a passion
Growing as time increases
Into the night I see
The ground still echoing underneath
Racing shadows
Attempting to hide their secrets
We have evaporated
We have evolved
The time has come to set a course
Into the opening world
I fight for what's before me
For what I've already had
Surroundings fade
Something has prompted the light
Artificial as it may seem
I must be done with the night
I can no longer avoid being seen
As it marches to sleep without me
I'm left with a world of ideas
Most of them orbit around you
In this ministry constructed
A line is drawn somewhere
I must shut it down
Even though we move on
I must push for rest
For we are on the verge
Of a new day's challenge
We stand back in awe of everything
As it all begins before us

LAST STEP

Shooting at stars with pebbles
I watch them all burn out
Marveling at my feat
Unknowing it was just their time

Trying to grow flowers with cyanide
Lifting peace on my shoulders
While rifles, napalm and missiles sit at my side

You've treaded water for both of us
As I've experienced the deep
I'm longing for home

Climbing these stairs for as long as I have memory
The top is now within sight
I've been hoping to take the last step for years
This is my opportunity to abandon all of my fears

HERE

First season's frost
First snow of the year
The first vengeance of fear
She is here with me

Reminiscence of days behind
Anticipation of tomorrow's sunrise
In my arms
She is here with me

Here with me
Not on some deserted island
While I'm adrift on an iceberg
In the middle of the sea

World as distraction
Selfishness as reaction
To make one correction
Is to keep her here with me

HOLD ON THE PAST

The city hums a calming tune
After the latest squall
Rendered invisible
Until I feel like they do

The stillness stares back
Blankets me with silence
There is peace
Without distinction

I never believed before
Too many improbabilities
I didn't want to be proven wrong
I didn't think I could be

I didn't yearn for a way of life
That I didn't think I needed
I thought it was for the feeble
I thought it was for the lost

It had to be right
Before I sought to maintain
Like an ambush I am buried
In warmth and comfort

Time is now my collaborator
Constructing answers out of questions
I may be self-protective
I'm just watching out for my heart

You've broken more ground
Than anyone before
Now it's time to regulate
And relinquish my hold on the past

RUN WITH SCISSORS

This is my condition
Disorganized resolution
Carefully preparing my mistake
By calling it a solution

A union with carelessness
In the mind of the controller
When we run with scissors
We may end up getting stitches

I'm not on the dark side
I've just finally seen the light
The images are still palpable
In the battle for what is right

I'm not casting judgment
I'm defending the choices I've made
My eyes are open for the first time
I feel my dissolution fade

Night's shadow was cast
Tomorrow takes a final bow
In a day you changed my life
Resolution is now

Something so beautiful
A landscape finally uncovered
A wish finally granted
You are my revelation

Lying in the field
Of your genetic make up
Vulnerability and confidence
I will treasure this as long as I have memory

CORNER OF THE WORLD

You call for the defensive
I covet to be the one
Delicate and fragile
Unexposed

I acquire the burden
If we can call it that
On the open road at dawn
To reach you by day
If this is how to thrive
The endeavor will be made
I take pleasure reaching
Into your corner of the world

I'm listening for you
Your voice is in my head
Waiting for your every move
Your words eradicate my indecision

Perfect other by no means suspected
Time and road no interference
Keep me in your mind as we interpret
How this will evolve

MINEFIELDS

They create a word and live by it
Expecting others to do the same
Some spend their life looking
It never amounts to anything
He creates his war from lies and fragments
While they create peace in all facets
Others stand with an open mind
Wondering what it would be like to just listen
She lives her life within herself
It's what makes her happy
He lives his life for someone else
It's who he wants to be
He has a job he detests
Yet he is home with family when it matters
She has a job she enjoys
But never sees them
Both can see the world
Both would not change a thing

Over there they are poor
Across the street they are wealthy
You don't miss what you never had
Something learned in time
Some hear one side
Then turn away
There are those who know the enemy
Then end up in the same delusion

It's a matter of diffusing the bombs of lies
In the minefields of what is true
It is what brings meaning in the end
I'm just glad I could love you

PARALLEL

Dressed up like a Vegas show
Down the street devils hide in shadows
Cry a little longer next time
For another's forlorn condition

Sleeping on clouds tonight
Tomorrow the resistance sets in
Someday everything will be all right
When our new arrangement begins

Parallel is the direction
We are parallel
All the uniform is parallel
Our future is parallel

A trip of nothingness
To reach everything
Sanity scans horizons
Horizons are deemed incompetent

Today I hear songs
When I turn the radio off
I have found clarity
In a world confused

You teach and challenge
Without words and action
I respond with timely precision
I find the world's secret passage

Smoldering is the flame of forgiveness
Turning in to a fire
Miles behind
Still visible in the distance

As I turn the corner
I see an outlying figure
Our paths have crossed for the first time
But our history appears similar

Parallel we two align
Parallel is our past and permeation
Our future lines up parallel
This is cause for celebration

SIT IN SILENCE

I would rather sit in silence
Than talk with anyone else
I always breathe much easier
With you around

For now I am able to forget
That you will leave again
Only to return on another day
As we wait to turn the tide in our favor

The day is approaching
When two worlds collide
Until that day there is speculation
So we choose to sit in silence

BELIEVE

She said I believe in trust
I believe in hope
I believe in you
I believe in us

Whatever gets you through
Whatever you have to hold on to
I believe in everything
I believe in you

If conviction gives you proof
That our encounter has been planned
Believe in what you want
Believe what you can

I believe in faith
I believe in music
I believe in preordainment
I believe in distance from the past

If you believe in truth
And you believe in absolution
Then I believe in love
And I believe in you

THE FIRST TIME

The expedition ended here before
Walking through these fields
Opening these rusty doors
Relinquishing the policies of natural laws
I've scaled these buildings when they were too high to climb
Yet today feels like the first time

My heart beats faster
With each contemplation
My anticipation imperious
Never to this elevation

Remembering plenty of stages
Where I lost it all but knew I had more
The years haven't taken my conviction
As I reach a new pinnacle

Aware of what was in the offing
It never hit me on the head like this
There is providence in every sign
It feels like the first time

Today something intangible
Before was hallucination
A wishing of what could be
I tried to make it what I wanted
Today there is no pulling string
There is no maneuvering
Everything set in place
Preserved in this space

Unaffected by the duration
It's magnificent to be here
I'm one in a race of many
You gave everything when I didn't have any

Frightening the ghosts from my mind
Expelling the nightly haunting
Away in a separate frequency
Reserved for you and me

In theory it could be argued
That history is repeating
Never has it all fallen into line
This is the first time

NECESSARY PROCESS

Maybe you get what you want
Maybe the state is permanent
The support will always be there
Despite the outcome
I never realized barrenness
I thought one step was too many
Some decisions are convenient
When you've started over again

I'm reputed once more
Considering the stars at night
The green and blue in my life
Allows for piece of mind

A necessary process
The world wasn't my liability
Not everything was a decision
I was supposed to lose everything
I had to stand in obscurity
I thought I knew everything
I didn't know anything
A necessary process

I remember my reflection
Not so long ago
I see the person I was
Allowing the world to intervene
Waiting for the right time
To feel what I should feel
Accepting that being half alive
Also meant being half dead

A necessary process
A permanent state
A rambling mind
Given time to relate
A time to find myself
A time to give my heart
A time to feel what you and I truly are
A necessary process

ALL YOU HAVE TO DO IS ASK

Looking through the owners manual of my life
In a pursuit of authenticity
Ghosts I didn't distinguish
Doubts date back a half-life
Revelations I already had
Never admitting to myself

Anticipate awareness
That only time bestows upon me
The mind just works this way
Severance of truth and fiction is a task
If there is ever something you need to know
All you have to do is ask

OXYGEN TANK

Thank you to my oxygen tank
To breathe in the dark oceans
In the depths of space
Strength for the future

The light overhead hangs like hope
The seasons pass through fear's onset
The arc of your voice
When you say nothing
I begin making my escape
No path to the sun
I cannot catch my breath
With my oxygen tank left behind
I have no more energy left
I no longer want to run

LOVE KNOWS NO TIME

Whirlwind of irresolution
In an era of war
She waves him goodbye
Neither knowing what for

Storm in her eyes
More bitter than before
Has now come to rise
In the vastness of their shore

You remain in the shadows
Hiding behind your door
Never where they are
Never anything more

Divine will in your stare
A disciple of truth
A part of reason and labor
Vengeance is yours

Anger and dejection
Turning into hate
She'd hoped to stand behind you
Now it's much too late

Infection of the brain
Taking over the rest
Wrapping around the heart
Beating in her chest

Fighting against hate
Still committing the crime
She holds onto belief
Love knows no time

Protest filled moment
Common bonds now absent
Heads hiding in the sand
Hatred is persistent

Co-existence
Before God stepped in
Long before attention changed focus
Delegating what is sin

Unbroken bond shields their eyes
A beautiful love in disguise
Evil lurks outside
Hatred dressed to kill

A union remains shared
Blurring the dividing line
Hate with no choice but to die
Love knows no time

SEAMLESS WITH THE HORIZON

The ocean drowns in her eyes
Seamless with the horizon
My restraint a catharsis
To the wound in my skin

She is a replenishing energy
I admonish going back
I believe it to be necessary
That this perpetuates

These lives are contiguous
This fate is imbrications
A new imperialism
Still in development

She is the last time
What is previous I extirpate
What is harmful I eradicate
What was broken I will mediate

NEXT TIME I WON'T ASK SO MANY QUESTIONS

I wasn't qualified to cross the line
I ran away from what I am
My head stayed behind to pick up the difference
I thought that only fools and liars existed here

In this realm of arrogance and complacency
I solidify my position
I look past realism
I take back my fear
I didn't want the world to change
Just my place in the line

We served as each other's permit
Meeting in the center of mystification
The outcome meant different things
We can still look at each other

Now I face being without you
Returning to my normal life
I will always remember
As long as memory allows
I had to know what you thought
So I knew how to feel
I was hoping you would provide suggestions
Next time I won't ask so many questions

ANNABELLE

I was waiting for life to assume its image
I blurted out control from a tower
A break into song by the voiceless
A fall into nothingness by those in power

In my journey of constant stalemates
Shot down by misfortune's events
Belief of life lived in high times
Only to discover constant descents

Annabelle you were fooled into thinking
That I ever knew the portion
Of my life that I was waiting for
But I never knew

Annabelle you waited for my number to be called
When you already had safe passage
To the next town where you were destined
That you now refuse to leave

I spend hours relinquishing control
As I'm eased into submission
A longing gaze into futures eyes
Confirms this is the right decision

Annabelle you knew of the times to come
Yet you never knew this is how our life would turn out
Now we face days in an event horizon
I finally know what my life is supposed to be about

I must have been on autopilot
My landing appears plotted out
All the signposts were foreign
Until I figured them out

Annabelle you are the capsule of time that I want to store
You are the face of a life that I've seen many times before
Now it has transcended the laws of time and of space
You are the revelation I no longer have to chase

All of the king's horses have stopped at your door
All tradition ceases and falls to your floor
Annabelle you are the image leading me to resolution
You are the icon that commenced my revolution

UNDYING

Drop me at the end of the ocean
Attempt to drown me in the sea
Miles before I'm forsaken
I will know it's undying

Lock me in a box for years
Catapult my mind to excessive thoughts
Sell my soul on the devil's market
Shatter my will to believe in anything
Still it is undying

Drag up the past in deceitful ways
Believe you know the scope of my mind
Attempt to hide the fear inside
Still it is undying

Wrestle the birds of flight
Eliminate the dark of night
Believe whatever you think is right
It is undying

Circumstances beyond control
Never the option in this world we own
Dealing in reality is the routine
Undying

Rest your head about your fear
I want to make something clear
Your loyalty is infinitely supplying
My love for you is undying

ORIGIN

The morning arrived quickly
This uprising
My old life races by
No time for reaction
No consciousness of interim
That this is how it is
And how it should be

Origin undetectable
It may have always been
It's better to travel well than to arrive
What really matters is the in-between

The old world disappears
New psychology evolving
I'm where I never thought I'd be
Now I don't want to leave

APOGEE

On this Indian summer night, I look to your stratosphere
We've been elliptical
We've reached the apogee
As far apart as we can get

My rotation slows
My vision clouded
I have no atmosphere left
Nothing is clear

My other side has been deceived
Vision changes in darkness
My return is predicted
It just takes time

At the furthest point
Our orbits cross for the first and only time
A culmination for the years of cold and darkness
We have reached our apogee for this lifetime

MEDITATION ROOM

ONE HOUSE LEFT STANDING SECTION II

A DISCOVERED JOURNAL

I stand around
I grow
The world expands around me
My leaves fall to the ground
I'm scaled
I'm observed
Some days I can barely breathe
My family, acquaintances, surroundings all gone
Somehow I survive
You move the earth around me
Burying your sins with lies
You cut them down as long as they're not in your back yard

Might as well send me packing too
There is nothing left for me here
I'm 10 times your life
As you think you're superior
One day you will perish by killing yourselves off
I will still be here

WINGS

A light source
A circadian sense
Hardwired knowledge
In the wavelength of the sun

Polarized illumination
Vibration in one plane
Never other directions
Photoceptors dominate my eyes

I detect the sun's angle
Even on a cloudy day
The ultraviolet luminosity
Always heading south

It is my sun compass
On the wings of my prayer
By the waves of knowledge unbenounced
I will always get there

MOTHER EARTH

My back faces the formation
I feel the calm cooling
Leading up to the final storm
We are not ready

Sins of violence and negligence
To assume control
Trampling hearts to succeed
Actions always justified

A priest with a bible in one hand
Holds an Uzi in the other
Preaching the way to millions
Losing his own

All possessions can be lost
There are no excuses you can use
The world is not for your disposal
Or to protect only when you choose

We need to handle with care
There is no more room for regret
Some might look the other way
But Mother Earth will never forget

WHERE ROADS END

I've heard the wind blow
Without the sounds of roads, power lines and engines
If you want to take that away
If buildings and concrete are your goal
Count me out

Land may be ice
Some still call it home
How could you know anything?
You haven't lived a hard day in your life
If you want to be praised for this progress
Count me out

I live where roads end
I hope it's more than that
In my dreams I know it can be
I have to believe something
I can't look at what you're building
When I can see what you're destroying

BANDA ACEH (To end all others)

The day after Christmas
A message sent and received
26 a special number
Fear of all that we know

Take your love for one another
Hold it in close
We are the survivors
In a day to end all others

Look out at the Indian Ocean
Question your Gods at this port haven
Never have we been more recognized
How soon we'll have been forgotten

BLOCKING OUT THE SUN

This city lot obstructs our view
Metal and glass to the sky
Depriving my piece of mind
Taking time that could be mine

All of this pressure
One day it just stops
I'm not here anymore
I'm tired of blocking out the sun

You take more than is fair
Emptiness in its place
You speak of integrity
When integrity is what you lack

The blood of my fore fathers
Taints the markings of fate
Blinds those that have never lost sight
Only initiating hate

You might be wearing the suit
It doesn't mean it fits
You've stabbed in the back for respect
It's the only thing you will never get

Someday you'll try astuteness
Your true colors will fly
Mediocrity at it's best
Your whole life is a lie

PRIVATE LAND

Where I'm going I have no indication
I have never felt appreciation
For anyone who thinks land is their private nation

You claim your defense
A scenario not making sense
Please offer another pretense

I'm only here for the view
I see you have nothing better to do
Than to call this your private land

Bureaucracy is ignorant
What's broken is surely bent
A sign shouldn't provide consent

We end up killing again
Then wonder where peace and love has been
It will be here longer than you can defend

No ground should be off limits
Sand is still sand
Even on your private land

BUYING A TICKET TO DIE

I used to believe that nothing could be premeditated
Now the days are too different and similar
Planned measures command a thought every week
Time reserved as soon as time is available

How did you get on board with this alliance?
Did you know this day would be yours?
Is there a way to rationalize stories untold?
Can we explain how something sudden can gradually unfold?

You need to buy a ticket to die
A certain time and place
So we in life have sufficient time
To fit in the saying of grace
You don't deserve any grievances
We don't have time to mourn or pray
If you're going to buy a ticket to die
You must do so today

The other day I saw a man
Older than the stars
Clothes and soles worn thin
Begging at passing cars
At the ticket counter
I kept my place in line
Later I picked up my planner
And scheduled a time to cry

My wife and I have settled
We know of no other way
The kids are gone and we've seen it all
There is nothing left for us to say
We look on to the future
Three weeks at a time
Maybe we'll plan our love and enthusiasm
Somewhere down the line

A long time coming
But you've gone and disappeared
Running with your piece of mind
Your emotional account has been cleared
It was not in the cards or on schedule
You didn't run it by me for approval
I had too much on my plate at the time
You need to warn me in the future

It's all turned to black and white
Sentiment has been removed
It is like numbers and figures today
It's much easier that way
Next time give me a warning
Or I will not jump through hoops
I need to make a good showing
And pretend I care about these troops

These days you have to buy a ticket to die
A certain time and place
So those of us in life have time
To be something other than two-faced
You don't deserve any grievances
We don't have the time to mourn or pray
If you're going to buy a ticket to die
You must to so today

BACK DOOR (for Ken)

This land was my land
This home was my home
I still feel a chill in the air
Bordering the warm naive glow of youth
I was always hopeful
Even when you sent me falling to the floor
I looked up to see God on stand by
Giving me daggers to live for more
But no key to the back door

This memory always there
In the back door of my mind
I was able to get away
Somehow still left behind
I stood at the back door
I could see the key in my mind
I look back to see him moving towards me
Feeling like eternity

As I was recaptured
I cursed fate for being so vindictive
To give me the likeness
But not the means to be free
Maybe there is a larger plan
Maybe I suffered through the world
To share my wisdom
Maybe I wouldn't know what to live for
Had I found the key and opened the back door

Years later I stand before you
A truce of sorts on both sides
Capitulation on the inside
Absolution and exodus
This was once my home
Now uninhabited
As if we traded places
After years of trying to forget

I stand here with these images
Lingering to this day
Causing me to leave this city, this state
And go my own way

Now God is front and center
I found you and I found significance
I find my way back here today
To give these memories a proper burial

The key was left on the patio
Every thing else taken away
In a ray of light I see my closure
As I opened the back door today

TO MY THREE GRUDGES

I was asked to dig in the dirt
In a head that tries to forget
Everyone that left
Anything that hurts

I dug back 18 years
I held a sanctimonious ruling over you
Like who you are then is who you are now
I could falter, be cold and judgmental
But you couldn't make a solitary mistake

I faded in and out
Leaving you to fill the spaces
I took and never gave
Today I'm apologetic

What becomes of someone who bites the hand that feeds?
I never pictured myself with that decree
I shut down because you called me out
Casting the line and leaving the bait
I never thought you'd try to gut me
I didn't want to arbitrate
I didn't want to hear details
I didn't want to feel the hate
I couldn't think of a position
That would've made me want to stay
Please know that nothing has changed
I had to get away
There is love and doubt as I extricate
I know time heals all wounds
I'll always hope for the best of outcomes
When I think of you

I thought I didn't do enough
I was blamed for pushing and pulling
You never realized how big of a factor everything was

The time has come to disavow and disintegrate
As I start over again
There is only so much giving to do
Until the focus turns inward

Please remember I miss being irresponsible
I want to be a child every day
I want to take your hands and stall your aging
I want to reverse time so we can rely on each other again

I'm sorry I haven't been more
But we are still alive
There shouldn't be any more excuses
I will forgive

Now we meet for the first time
I thought my mind finally captured happiness
At least I was hoping
Moving too quickly
Yet this grudge seems to have lasted the longest

You were in one ear and out the other
Before I could get the message
I was your first oversight, apparently
I fit the role of victim
I've rehearsed it time and again

It's been weighing me down
I wanted you to feel something
You insisted you were the casualty
That needed time to heal

To this day I don't have an answer
This story has a cliff-hanger conclusion
For you there is no culpability
Apart from what you think you should feel

That's not something I want from you
No words without authenticity
It's a matter of living with yourself
If only I believed that

My position is evasion
As I give you power
You're indifference has left me abandoned
My torture was not letting it go

It's time to take off the blindfold
I don't want to fuel that fire anymore
The slate will be clean
As the weight falls from my shoulders

I don't care that you are out there anymore
I don't care if you never fess up
I'm not validating my manic state by blaming it on you
It's been too easy for too long
This has been harmful to everyone
I've escaped the demise without your help
I'm stronger without you than you'll ever be alone
I gave you all the credence that you thought you deserved
My persona fed your illness
Your lack of it created mine
I'm not wasting any more time on you
I've broken free of the chains around my wrists and heart
I've left the heavy load outside my realm of consciousness
Maybe on some dark day it might sneak in from time to time
But it will never be worth it

I know how to put this to rest
I'm finally free of everything you should be feeling
I wasn't always there for you
I didn't do all that I could
I wasn't the best at telling you everything
I don't think it would have mattered anyway
I forgive you for what I could not
I forgive myself for my part
Now we've come to terms
Me and this imaginary you
If I look back it will be with a smile
I'll laugh at what we've been through

So my love here we are
Post destruction and chaos
One thousand words spoken
A million more unsaid

Lately my head has been clear of the identity it's taken
It's been able to focus on a solitary thought
I'm starting to feel through the numbness again
As the rebuilding slowly begins

I look ahead to see opportunity
In my dreams I see you there
We've made it through the worst of storms
With some sanity to spare

Even though parts have gone up in smoke and fire
The core remains in tact
Just remember everything before is fiction
Remember that we are fact

THICKER

I've cleansed myself in sand and mud
My lies have stood taller than my truths
I've led the blind masses
Hate has made more sense than love

I've forgiven you for throwing daggers
My wounds are still bleeding
This path is because of you
It is who I've become

Weak muscles are strengthening
Distance causes healing
Time stands against the time before
Innocence is not the same as ignorance

A tree in need of nourishment
You'd never allow growing a bud
I tried to explain the reasons why
It doesn't do any good
I'd hoped you'd acknowledge the boundary lines
Even though you never would
I thought you'd honor fidelity and reason
As you claimed everyone else should
This is why my life has taught me
Water is thicker than blood

CUT AND DRY

It is impossible to test the weather
With a broken barometer
It's hard to see the big picture
Wearing your blinders

You know but you don't know
You've seen what is before you
You haven't lived it out
Life isn't always cut and dry

There isn't always right and wrong
There isn't always an obvious path
Not every main road leads to happiness
Not every road can take you back

Life is peaks and valleys
As it stalls and fumbles before you
The race has begun but you haven't left
The only truth is what you see

Quiet the conversation enough
To tell you what is happening
The judgment falls before your eyes
Until you consider the other side

You've taken all the right steps
You haven't lived the alternate
You feel the need to decide
Even though you've never fallen

Sanctimony is an ugly color
You haven't put on another's shoes
You think that life is cut and dry
That this could never happen to you

One day you will find yourself stranded
All you've denied and rejected in me
Will come back to catch you at the heels
You will know how stringency feels

Until that day I wait and wonder
How your unawareness has augmented
I'm sorry you cannot see the spell you are under
Life is never just cut and dry

CRYSTALIZED

For years you submersed yourself in domestication
Until its welcome wore out
Now it's tearing where it matters most
Like a glove that does not fit

You try to reflect familial dedication
Never convincing the one that matters most
The recognizable shortsighted enemy rises
Rearing its head once again

If you were dragging yourself down
It would be open and shut
For you it takes two fools
One bigger than the other
A wizard of self-trickery
As you attempt self-mockery
A practice you've perfected
By avoiding self-imagery

The painter of a picture
Depicting everyone else as crazy
It might hold water
If there was no such thing as reason, reputation or history
It takes a lot of courage
To be such a coward
Someday the light will fade
Those around you will no longer be blinded

Your promises have become crystallized
Far too many times
Along with it the victims
As well as the crimes

POSITIVE TRAITS

Simplicity no longer effective
No slouching on the tight rope
No more taking the low road
No more of who I was

You consider all you are
All I should be to you
The last thought in your mind
While reading the devil's handbook

I've been the escape artist
I've hit every existing wall
Every time I've tried to miss
There is no other way through

Irony or fate
You don't get the time of day
Of course you can't see it my way
Excuse my limited positive traits

Hold my confidence for ransom
Use it for your last bit of sanity
Maybe this is your empowerment
That is all it will ever be

SINNER & SAINT

Stones upon your grave
The world's mistake all over your face
Whatever words I speak
Always you're the victim

Historically preserved in a case
Spectators gasp in awe
A reluctant commonwealth from the start
Now in ruins

In the dead of night
Cause finds effect
Sanity reunited
Forgiveness finds regret

Gloominess gathers
Congregating in the sky
It rains, then dissipates
The sun alone once the clouds break

A matter of principal
Emotional reaction under restraint
Refusal to be walked over again
You're the sinner, I'm the saint

Left as a mystery
Importance disregarded
Overlooked by brain scholars
Presently discussed in dignity's final hours

PRESENCE OF STRANGERS

Standing in knee deep snow
Funnel clouds surround me from above
Allegedly with family
None of them do I know

I attempt to take shelter
I try to climb but I sink deeper
Staggering through uncertainty
Moving in the wrong direction

I relocate to the heart of the storm
Nothing they can appreciate
Hostility and judgment surround me
Welcoming me home again

Here I find my only familiarity
Nothing they could ever recognize
I spent a lot of life walking backwards
Offering apologies for their oversights

A stranger used my eyes to see
As the well was running dry
I will not stand in your shadow
That's consumed with self-righteousness

I cannot shape silence
To make words you want to hear
I've been the hero, mistake and downfall
Now it's time for me to become whole

THE DISAPPEARING CHILDREN

Morning field glistens
Before dew evaporates
Imprisoned by my own hand
Watching the slow progression
Memories of playing in the fields
Like a child today
Once there were no thoughts or options
Once it was just reaction

Giving way to accountability
Dissolving our innocence
Preparing to lay the groundwork
So they can play in the same fields

No happiness in servitude
Altruism only goes so far
There has to be a better way
Without giving your soul

I think back to these fields
I see your face devoid of anxiety
Optimism the only option
It's just part of the game

We were the same children
I see them everyday as I go by
I turn to walk away
When I look back they are gone

IDEA

We stand and fall
A concept driven into our minds
A hat or a crown above our heads
It's an idea

Dug into the world's wheel treads
A glimmer remaining where the sun used to set
We watch the moon fall from our sky
An idea whose time has passed us by

We attempt to steal the remaining praise
But hope vanished in the previous phase
We rebuild from the ground up
Only time will tell if it is enough

Looking through these tired pages
A war of boys still wages
No consistent ideology to embrace
We need an idea to set the pace

A million faces as one
Waiting for an explanation for what's been done
A reestablishment of what has begun
Maybe it's an idea whose time has come

ONE REASON

Magical potions creating wonder
Like a sniper throwing cannonballs
A penchant for pillorying
In a descendant kind of way

Statements of animosity
Between the first and second one
Rendering the elder incoherent
Vindicating the son

The hand -me- down makes the difference
Improving the path to victory
Taking the antiquated procedure
Revolutionizing effortlessly

The slowest of leaks
Finally causes the flood
Determination lassos hope
Like they knew it could

No more hiding, no more lies
I'm not afraid to look to the sky
I hear what is spoken
I understand

No longer afraid to dig in the ground
Or paint a new idea
I'm a photograph waiting to be developed
So I can be set in this frame

The moon passes
The night is soft and welcoming
The first time I can close my eyes
That I know I will sleep

Hard-pressed wisdom and hope
Distances fall apart
Pulled together like cartoon cliffs with a rope
So we can make our way across

We came together for one reason
Way back when
Many pretend they didn't
They know the truth in the end

BIG STORY

Waiting and wondering
As if God prepared a speech
Then arranged to die
As if questions will be answered

It's another murky question
To something temporarily not soil
The electronic circus lies dormant
Waiting for another attack

The day is inevitable
The signs are in the air
The truth of immortality
Afraid of reality

It's passable to pursue demise
To make a life the tabloids
Death is a popularity competition
The universal follower avoids

They couldn't be more contented
Unless they caught a crucifixion on tape
The world is now in reverence
Allowing the crazy and misguided to escape

We might as well prepare for war
Making light of everything
Proceeding to sell your soul
As long as you're prepared for the big story

A PAUSE IN THE CONVERSATION

A free flowing argument
Words as weapons and tools
A consortium of intelligence
Criticizing the fools

An angle taken too far
One member bows out
As if deceit has run rampant
Taking a different route

There was a pause in the conversation
Like a riot in the street
A battle for composure
A proposal claiming defeat

Now the secret revealed
Tormenting is the solution
An unauthorized topic
Drives towards this conclusion

You may not know the half of it
Someone raised him in fear
The stories narrated to him
Were never reasonably clear

There was a pause in the conversation
A disturbance of one mind
Removal from betrayal
And any other excuse he could find

There was a pause in the conversation
Like a riot in the brain
Now he lives in fear
Of having to explain

JUST FOR SHOW

I'll stay by the light of the 28th stair
In the moon's glow where no one can see
After the words have hallowed out my soul
I'll stay here until piece of mind arrives
He remains downstairs
Until the weapons are put away
Until the wisdom is no longer absent
Until the light of the new day

Your words a reaction of thought and emotion
I heard nothing of truth after
I knew my place was not there
So here I will remain
Until the apology is besetting
Until the lies are convincing
Until answers are forthcoming
Until the warmth ushers out the cold
When the silence begets forgiveness

The distant sounds of horns pacify my head
I lay my fears aside
I try to keep what's mine
Casting out the remaining emptiness
The morning sun speaks
A new day is emerging inside me
No more staying here just for show
It's time to let the night go

THE PREMEDITATED

The old rerun replays
With you sitting in the chair
My thoughts grab me from behind
You don't notice my stare

I can't look at you and be happy
I can't look away and forget
You've polluted the good days of my life
Gambled away on a simple bet

If I should raise my voice
You raise a hand
Since you've become devil's advocate
No explanation is good enough

Turning on me is one thing
Taking her down is another
You can strike the wife right out of me
But you cannot take the mother

Frequency and intensity increase
Now I'm biding my time
Allowing this to be a way of life
Will be my only crime

A war enduring years
Has worn out its welcome
I'm through shedding tears
I'm prepared to create an outcome

Her week begins at school
Out of harms way
I fantasize about walking up to you
Or doing it in your sleep

I wait and let the well dry up
I rattle what little patience you possess
You ask the inevitable
So predictable I didn't have to guess

As you approach me for the last time
I'm ready for what's next
Only two and you're on the floor
You won't lay a violent hand on anyone anymore

TRUTH CRIES

It could be bad timing
Maybe you can breathe in and out
Right now that should be good enough
Until the temptation is gone

You go into shut down
You stand and fall
You sleep in the bed you made
With the writing on the wall

There is something better
Than a journey through living hell
You'll see it on the other side
Forgiveness for yourself

Give it a second thought
The first one forbids going back
There is no allowance for detraction
No room for mistake
The message is only the lesson
Only you can feel the weight
Self-contained without explanation
As you attempt to make your escape

I have no message to leave you
I have no wisdom to give
If you need purpose, look around you
The young eyes looking back at you
Should make you want to live
She'd be a fighter and a misfit
Until her day of reckoning calls
She will fall down or rise above
Only in spite of it all

It would be much easier
If you could accept you cause this pain
There are already difficult answers to give her
How could this one be explained?

I stand here at your mercy
The wave is much deeper than you realize
The echo would redefine sound
A form of logic, humor and reason dies
As truth cries

WASTE OF SPACE

No such thing as a favorite son
No such thing as a good gun
No words or sentiments to retract
The battle has already begun

I am not worthy of access
I do not think like you do
Do not speak of vengeance
As if you never knew

There is more at stake
Than a lie followed through
Be proud to show your face
Not just a waste of space

BLACK DOG

Black dog on the porch
You don't have the weight of life
You don't have a heart that's lied
You don't think the grass is greener on the other side

You run the trails you're given
Wearing the same path
You don't worry if love will die
Or who will suffer the aftermath

You don't want to fly
You don't want to fix those who are broken
Never needing to prove emotion
Your love is demonstrated without a word ever spoken

Teach me how to forgive
Show me how to let it go
Simplify the world before me
Black dog, teach me what you know

LEAVE OR STAY

You ease into fixation,
By singing nursery rhymes to devils
Words are your balustrade
Being forthcoming is arduous

The outer barrier appears welcoming
If it's not of importance then it's not you
Searching for some comfort
In the essence of sight you modify your mind
How many times do we save the composition?
Before it starts to crumble?
I fear the present and future
It's inevitable that I will stagger
Less life ahead than behind
I don't know if I could get away
Time to make up my mind
Whether I leave or stay

STANDING ON THE BANK OF A RIVER ON A SNOWY DAY

Standing on the bank of a river on a snowy day
My feet feel the earth through my shoes
I pull my hat down over my ears
I look out at the newly formed layers of ice

I heard things about you today
I came out here for peace and quiet
I thought it would be a good place to clear my head
I know the life you're leading by what others have said

It's not what you lied about; it's that you lied at all
A deliberate course of action
I have no further investments
I still can help to wonder

The snow increases its invasion of the ground
Hugging the spaces that keep the river warm
Neither the earth nor I make a sound
Just a spectator, performer, an art form, and the ground

Admiring the attention to detail
As it leaves nothing untouched
I think how you have been so careless
How I simply cared too much

Minutes turned into hours
Bringing a calm and acceptance
I know every snowflake will reach its destination
One lands in my hand before the snows duration

HER DIVINITY AND BEAUTY

She is the queen of my last empire
Her castle on a dead end street
She is the painting of the rift valley
In the moment where I soared overhead
Now the desert storm in my heart
Has initiated new beginnings
I always knew she'd end up in my mind

I could have loved her years ago
But I'm half the man I was
I could have loved her yesterday
But shadows bring ambiguity

Out of whole cloth and out on a limb
My sun God is burning bright
I've seen her divinity and beauty like three Graces
As I attracted the three Fates
Now three Furies know of my transgressions
I know I've lived my last day with her
I harm her for the last time

A fate cruel enough for history
That we could never be as one
My heart will always regret
I've caused a storm I cannot weather
She'll never know I'm sorry
My arms were meant to be around her
The harshest of punishments I will face

I'm in my darkest of times
I'm a stranger to myself
I don't know right from wrong
I'm someone who could hurt you like I did
Yet be unable to figure out how

I am outside myself looking in
As if I'm not causing this pain
My history is a monster
Moving in for the kill
Rightfully destroying my accomplishments
Taking one piece of my heart at a time
As I am pushing her away
Assuring her exit for the final time
When my only hope is for her to stay

A DREAM OF PAST AND PRESENT IN THE SAME BED

Standing on the border of reminiscence
Losing my footing on the rocks
Falling to the dangerous summit
Of genuine and imaginary

The past tried to be present
The old and new
You sought after a return
Making yourself at home

This bed is made
You have been hiding
You can't throw your hat in the ring
When there's no ring to throw it into

With your heart in hand
You taste your own medicine
The tide has turned
You must find your way

I will walk you home
It will be for the last time
Wipe the tears from your eyes
It's time to go forward

I have no feeling
I have no fears
It's far beyond me
To shed any tears
A dream of past and present in the same bed
Capable of conjuring a nightmare
I was able to handle it instead
Paying the heavy as you permanently exit my head

ALL THAT WAS ANYTHING

I tried to walk a straight line
Even when the walls were changing shape
The pictures remained the same
I could usually stay the course

I'd give you a hand
But I care not to raise a finger
You've succeeded with little effort
Expecting everyone to kneel before you

I was the floor
You walked all over me
I sense a line being drawn
In the direction of my favor

If I have a slate
It is wiped clean
The time has come
For your defense

There is no validation
No more excuses for reckless abandon
There is no sense to the lunacy
That you consider deliberate

A step closer to knowing
A step further from caring
You've done it to yourself this time
As you lose all that was anything

ANNOYANCE TO THE UNIVERSE

Jaded and discovered
Welcome worn out
No surprise or mystery
Just a smudge in history

One too many things spoken
Arrival at nowhere again
Care too much and you're blamed first
As the annoyance to the universe

Too invested and involved
Too close to the fire to see the ice
Juggling with way you are
And the way you want to be

It's impossible to follow
The path that is sorrow
Unresolved but it could be worse
Than being an annoyance to the universe

THE OTHER ONE

I'm the untilled wheat field
I'm the wind without a path
I've been the victim
I've been the culprit

I am both sides of the story
I'm missing the components of sympathy
I've been the love and the hate
I've betrayed for betrayal's sake

I abandon those I've supported
I pretend to be brave to hide the coward
I've stayed because I was too weak to leave
I left because I was too weak to stay

I used to be one, now I'm the other
I'm the giving and the taking
I'm the wanting and forsaking
I'm the real and the faking

FIGMENT

I raise my white flag on this day
As my enemies approach on every front
Mistakes are my debt, mostly paid

Hindsight proves I am weaker than I thought
What right do I think I have?
After hurting everyone who cared

I received more possessions than love
I disposed of hearts in need of protection
I ravaged all the calm waters in my head

You were marching forward and I brought you to a halt
Your love is sweet but mine tastes of salt
I tried to believe it wasn't my fault

Maybe I never knew what kept me going
Never missing the unknowing
Never looking into certainty with a confident eye

Love was always the one thing I thought I had
Walking on chains high above the clouds
Always so close to falling down

One hundred thoughts live in my mind
Never to see the light of day
One million excuses have been served

This entrapment keeps me moving in place
Severe punishment in every case
Sometimes it fit the crime

I would trade the world to be your hero
To take sorrow off your list
To meddle in this intricate philosophy

You deny this was sabotage to your heart's location
You say it's nothing more
Than a figment of my imagination

WARNING SHOT

She gave all the love in the world
To a partner in crime
In a foreseeable distance
That was becoming less foreseeable

The best kept secret was ignorance
Building upon itself for so long
Blanketing possibilities once open
Hoping to go home again

A random detected warning shot
The voiceless begin to speak
A sacrifice so I could see
Everything I am not

THE PRICE

I'm not here to meet you
I'm not on a journey for authenticity
I'm not here to thicken the plot
Nor to offer sincerity

Repetition can be costly
I don't drive on the same street for too long
I don't ignore my inner child
Nor wish I could prove you wrong

I like big words
I like myself a little too much
I haven't lived up to the billing
I'm not all I'm cracked up to be

One by one my silence crumbles
Nothing will ever suffice
Around and around I go again
Life is free, pain is the price

GUILT'S BED

It's just one step forward
With a vision in tact
To initiate action
Or change direction
Something as good as gone
Or left for dead
An old religion, an old song
Now abandoned in guilt's bed

Belief's turn is here
Included in the journey on this night
Hoping they buy into the prophecy
To finally make a difference
A long journey is ahead
With troubled times
It's bound to be worse
Before it gets better

Searching for a steady hand
To steady the boat
We all take for granted
That we've managed to stay a float
Hate is a superpower
Love is equally strong
Chasing fairy tails
When unity takes too long

No need to impose
Or to preach a life lesson
No one needs our help
To help them stop thinking
Uncertainty doesn't imply aggression
Patience doesn't breed fear
Just because they've turned a deaf ear
Doesn't mean they cannot hear

Waste away to nothing
Throw out common sense
Continue peaceful aggressions
Then be greeted by self-defense
A future on the rise
It's time to take a stand
If you want to help them
Just reach out your hand

DISTURB

I didn't get the message
For the nocturnal call of truce
Once a picture on the doorway
Now fallen and torn

Like the sky at the end of the world
I have finished this thought
It feels like an endless race
As I pass the call of failure

Inadequate time for importance
Extensions for trivial
I ride to the end of the day
Uncertain how to exist

I hate to disturb you
I never wanted to take this route
Searching for comfort
Before I'm the odd one out

From the edge I look down
I lose my footing and slip
Catching myself on the ledge
Ultimately losing my grip

The wind is cold on my face
It's you that goes through my mind
Until my very last day
It is you I cannot be without

The ground rapidly approaches
The moment hits me at last
No more wishing I can stay
My present is the past

You may think me disturbed
Our minds cross in the south
They have taken their final trip
As the words are seized from my mouth

The ending not like the start
Never promised as such
You still keep me unbroken
As the world threatens to be too much

THIS FOREST WON'T GROW

A whisper takes a thousand years to reach you
Numbness better left unsaid
Fear is a platform to anxiety
Coated with ignorance on the outside

This morning I stepped outside
I looked around in sadness
A land once flourishing is now dead
I should have believed the predictions

I wanted to be patient
I thought the word would spread
I tried to plant the seeds of love and understanding
This forest won't grow

SO BEGINS THE FLOOD

The crystal ball tells the story
Denying future remedies
Caustic fumes burn our insides
A war of water and fire set to begin

The puddle outside
Evidence from the rain of continents
As the storm's center approaches
The prediction is proven true

The rain falls harder

So begins the flood
Overflow of the channels
Pouring into hearts
Settling into lungs

Seeking the mistaken identity
Incongruity no longer ignored
Prepared for lethal force
Before civil action runs its course

Beheading a foreign policy
Claiming determination
As no one lifts a finger
Another one is lost

And the rain falls harder

Settle in the trenches
For a long night of redundancy
The eyes closing
Hope the morning brings resolve

We're still in the same chapter
With fists full of rain
A driving force
As the future takes course

The rain falls harder

The route of over-confidence
Over-estimation of importance
The flood reveals our insignificance
A last breath gasped in disbelief
A thousand years from now
The rain begins again
With it, a fossil resurfaces
A new race studies their discovery
To learn from our mistakes
Before the flood comes again

STOP PRETENDING

Months have now passed
Since this repercussion
The ground lay barren
Miles of devastation

There is a considerable distance
Before evidence of life
Everyone buried in their own place
Unaware of their lack of attention

I remember the fall out
Transgressions now archaic
Nothing is attainable
No way to force communication

Time a ticking bomb
Misfortune is the allied enemy
Within the tombs of ignorance
Lay the silhouettes of the past

Disintegrations of a lie
Though much worse than speaking outright
Solitary, though surrounded
Perceptible, yet out of sight

Still probing for words
To build our institution
To speak on the same level
To break down the towering walls

I have nothing more invested
There is still no comprehending
I'm not at wits end anymore
So we can stop pretending

TIME

Time hasn't settled your bets
The image of you comes into focus
I see into your life
With the fewest of words

You give the positive
Withhold the negative
Overpoweringly subtle
I see the difference
Hollow the dissatisfaction
After full disclosure
As close as it gets
Before time heals wounds

I can't think of anything more
I don't have words for you
I'd rather keep you guessing
Than return the favor

A mask wearing happiness
Distilled by reality
Buried by embarrassment
Hidden by semblance of pride

Go about your business
Into the misty morning
Time may have not settled anything for you
But it served you right

TWO HARDEST THINGS

To stop this runaway train
I lay across the tracks
I grab the steering wheel
But I'm a reckless driver

Still straight ahead and uniform
After the changing of guards
My inner compass turning
Away from your magnetic pull

I thought it was the end of hope
The straw that breaks the back
The last star at night
The last ides of March

Carnivorous emotions
Track the scent of my good nature
Feasting on my contentment
Warding off my integrity

My misanthropic behavior
Searching for the source
Designed to distract
The basis of longevity

I see it for what it's for
I fought off the truth
I know I was livid
For all the wrong reasons
As I reach the final stretch
On the road that I call patience
Of Avenues named desolate
Of passages through abasement

After enough humiliation
Pride is all but gone
The two hardest things
That I've ever had to do
Is admitting you were right
And admitting I was wrong

NOT ALWAYS WHAT THEY SEEM

Two times I would've walked a thousand miles
To stand a single day
Here on the mountains of dilemma
My artificial colors show
My mind welcomes nothingness
My heart no longer holds its note
I'm facing the opposite direction
At an ending I've never seen before

My stake is in the earth
I've traveled here with my possessions
Losing track of my identity
The story you read about me is true

It's easiest to run and hide
I'm best at deflecting affection
When the time comes to turn the tide
I'll be running in the other direction

Emotions are all the same
It's what's done in between
I'm the perfect example
Things are not always what they seem

CLARIFICATION

I won't ignore what is said and done
Or who knows the limitations
Don't get into a war of words
Because you will lose
I know your politics are yours
I know you have a lifetime of justification
I'm not trying to change the world
I just need some clarification

It's only been a while
I'm parked here in your station
Awaiting the next chance I get
To receive an invitation
There's love and trust
With wartime invasion
Driving us both forward
Seeking intimidation

As we settle inward
We experience the coronation
It is everything I've ever wanted
Thank you for this clarification

I WILL NOT BE CONTAINED

You wish you may you wish you might
Try to label me
Methods could serve your conscience
In the prison of your ways

I cannot live in that box
All my life I've refrained
You will serve a different future
I will not be contained

Stop with the demands
Don't assume you run with what is right
Age and wisdom don't come into play
When you're always a step behind

I will not put on that lock
Outside of commodity I've remained
I've broken the shackles and now I can run
I will not be contained

In several years your soul will be lost
After treating it with disdain
Was it worth the cost?
I will not be contained

15TH ROAD

Repetitive sound from deviations
Leaving the land of make believe
The worst of weather is over
Another chapter will close

The cyclical continuation
Of hypnotizing comforts
In a world of trees and silence
Here on 15th road

I have thoughts of you
This road is not long enough
The past has many avenues
Where truth was hidden from sight

I didn't exist in certainty
It didn't exist in me
I'd forgotten what it was like to remember
When I was more than just a need

The sky above is a wonderful distraction
Words would only ruin the moment
Words create belief
Words create war
Words set us apart
Words become our downfall

This road was built long ago
No life is seen here today
This is the appeal
The reason there's piece of mind

UP TO ME

Missing the boat for some time
A step short of discovery
The missing page in a novel
That contains the big reveal

A captain without a boat
Drowning in waves of convenience
Boasting about ignorance
Claiming to have credentials

Hoping the tide will turn
That the pieces will fall into place
Maneuvering behind the scenes
Now it is up to me

Wading into the water
Feeling the warmth of all that's been written
The review of history tells no surprises
The future is up to me

NEW FOUND ILLUMINATION

Too little freedom is prison
It's the same with too much
My readers are confused by now
In their search for consistency

For the longest time I was lost
I hated where I was
I hated where I ended up
I hated who I'd become
I didn't know myself
I was afraid to find out
Passiveness served me better
Hoping the world left me behind

I put the distance between us
The enemy and myself
The contradiction and challenge
The truth and reality

The weight I carry is no longer a burden
My knees are no longer weak
The path is no longer dark
My mind's eye no longer closed

Complicate or compliment
Everything appears to make sense
It's time to stop seeking indignation
And embrace the new found illumination

LEARNING TO FLY

All the grievances for the century
Bound in the secrecy of the current
Trees no longer accept the wind
Only stillness remains

Under the oppressive heat
This barren land grows life
A spitting image of truth
In a year of remembrance

I see the flight path before me today
I have faith it will extend into tomorrow
There is always another pattern to follow
As I learn to fly

Far away from home
I hear echoes of what's left behind
Straddling the straight line of congruence
Discovering that everything changes

This time my life turned for the better
I felt the gusts under my wings
The burst of energy below me
It's what the confluence of life brings

I've been led astray
Never to wonder why
To all those I've hurt, it's in this new story I plan to remain
It's all part of learning to fly

DISTANCE AND TIME

Where shadows have been cast I now want light
These are new rules
What once applied is now thrown out
Distance and time

Unexpected
Undeterred
A light with all the bulbs burnt out
Illuminating every step

I want to repeat to you
All of the hackneyed lines
Everything now graces my heart
Distance and Time

Long the winter before
The essence of a thousand years
Long the time in waiting
Foreshadowing whispers

A pleasant surprise
With nothing left to prove
No more to give or so it once seemed
Until it turned unexpectedly

At first an adversary
Then a familiarity
Soon you know you are sold
On distance and time

Wondering what comes next
Decisions are now queried
Old methods disposed
Uprooting the proverbial
Embracing a given path

Thankful once and for all
As confusion makes its curtain call
Knowing everything has fallen in line
It becomes so much more
After distance and time

TIME TO MOVE ON

I've been in prison
I thought you were the reason
The chains were of my making
Holding me down

This is no longer power
There is nothing more you can acquire
I won't hold out for answers anymore
It's time to move on

I wasn't there when I should have been
Then I wore out my welcome
A ceremony speaks to end it all
It's time to move on

Here we are, looking back
At the years under our microscope
We turn to face the new day
As one journey is ending

I've become the good in you
You've become the good in me
Repetition of reactions now broken
It's time to go home

Looking forward, we recognize
Much of the painful history is gone
I love you more than anything
It's time to move on

Thank you for reading...

THE END

www.ingramcontent.com/pod-product-compliance
Lightning Source LLC
LaVergne TN
LVHW011246080426
835509LV00005B/644